information the store 📞01603 773114
email: tis@ccn.ac.uk

Mike Wilson

Published in association with The Basic Skills Agency

Hodder & Stoughton

A MEMBER OF THE HODDER HEADLINE GROUP

Acknowledgements
Photos: pp. 2, 5, 7, 15 and 21 © Action Images.
pp. 11 Colorsport.
pp. 17, 27 © msi.
Cover photo: © Action Images

Orders: please contact Bookpoint Ltd, 39 Milton Park, Abingdon, Oxon OX14 4TD. Telephone: (44) 01235 400414, Fax: (44) 01235 400454. Lines are open from 9.00–6.00, Monday to Saturday, with a 24 hour message answering service. Email address: orders@bookpoint.co.uk

British Library Cataloguing in Publication Data
A catalogue record for this title is available from The British Library

ISBN 0 340 701064

First published 1997
Impression number 10 9 8 7 6 5 4 3 2
Year 2004 2003 2002 2001 2000 1999 1998

Copyright © 1997 Mike Wilson

Typeset by Fakenham Photosetting Ltd, Fakenham, Norfolk.
Printed in Great Britain for Hodder & Stoughton Educational, a division of Hodder Headline Plc, 338 Euston Road, London NW1 3BH by Page Bros, Norwich.

Contents

1 One kick too far

Wednesday, January 27, 1995.
The night Eric Cantona will remember for ever.
The night his life changed for good.
This was the night that Cantona,
the genius of French football,
went one kick too far.

Cantona was playing for Manchester United,
against Crystal Palace, at Selhurst Park.
Twelve minutes into the second half,
he was sent off for kicking a Palace player.
It was Cantona's fifth red card of the season.

He walked from the field with his head down,
as the crowds jeered all around him.
Suddenly, he turned and jumped into the crowd.
He kicked a Crystal Palace fan in the chest.
He then tried to punch him.

Why did Cantona act the way he did?
Would Cantona ever play in England again?
Would he ever learn to control his temper,
and mend his ways?

His story begins in 1966.

There is no doubt that Eric is a brilliant player. However, his temper has often got him into trouble.

2 Beginning

He was born on May 24, 1966,
in Marseille, in the South of France.

His father's family came from Sardinia.
His mother's family came from Spain.

In his early life,
the family lived in a large one-room cave
just outside Marseille.

From the age of five or six,
Eric played football for the local youth team.
Even at that age,
everyone knew he was special.

He was fast,
he could play in any position.
He could pass well, with both feet,
and he was very intelligent as a player.

One of his early coaches described him:

'He was different.
He had more intelligence than the others,
he was a level above them.
He knew when to hold the ball,
when to pass it.
He knew how to use it
to do something positive . . .'

But the temper was already there.

The coach of his youth team called him:

'Hot-headed, but a genius.
He knew he was better than anyone else.'

One of his early heroes was the Dutch star,
Johan Cruyff.
Another was kung-fu fighter, Bruce Lee.

Eric joined his first professional football club
when he was 15.

He played for six French clubs,
including his home town, Marseille,
before coming to England.

He was soon famous,
for being a genius.
He was also famous
for being a hot-head.
If his team didn't win,
or if Cantona wasn't playing well,
trouble was never very far away.

Once, he got in a fight
with his own goal keeper.
Cantona gave him a black eye.

Then he threw his boots
into a team-mate's face.

Eric in 1984 when he was playing for Auxerre in France.

3 Problems

Once, when the crowd was jeering him,
he lost his temper.
He kicked the ball into the stand,
tore off his shirt and threw it on the ground.

Another time he threw the ball at the referee,
then left the pitch
without waiting for the red card.

The French Football Federation had a hearing
to discipline Cantona.
He went along the line of officials,
calling each one 'idiot' to his face.

He was banned for two months.

When Eric played for the French national team,
it was the same story.
He helped France to some famous victories,
especially against Spain and Germany.
At one time he scored nine goals
in 11 internationals.

But then he went and spoiled it all,
by swearing at the French national coach
and calling him
'one of the most incompetent managers
in world football.'

Eric holding the French Cup in 1990. He was playing for Montpelier at the time.

The French Football Federation
had another hearing
to discipline Cantona.

He was banned again.

Cantona's brilliant playing
helped win the French Cup
for his club team Montpelier.

But often he was moved on loan,
from club to club,
when his behaviour let him down.
He had no discipline.

The Marseille manager sold Cantona
for half what he'd paid for him.
It was all getting too much for Cantona.
On December 12, 1991,
he retired from football in France.
He'd had enough.
He was 25.
He was still a brilliant player.
But within a month,
he wanted to come back.

Cantona missed football too much.
He couldn't live without it.
The trouble was, he couldn't play in France.
No manager would have him back.

So Eric Cantona came to England.

4 Sheffield Wednesday

The first club Cantona joined,
in July 1992,
was Sheffield Wednesday.
The deal lasted one week.

Wednesday's manager, Trevor Francis,
was very keen to sign a genius like Cantona.

But he was also careful.
He wanted to try the Frenchman
for one week.
He wanted to make sure that Cantona
would get on with his new team mates.

Cantona felt insulted.
He felt he was being given a test
and called the Sheffield Wednesday deal off.

5 Leeds United

Howard Wilkinson,
who was the manager of Leeds United,
did not hesitate.
He was not as careful as Trevor Francis.

He phoned Cantona,
and talked to him.
He asked him to delay his flight
back to France.

Cantona agreed.
They met the same day, January 31, 1992.
Within a few hours,
Eric Cantona signed for Leeds United.

It took Cantona some time
to settle in to the English game.

It was faster, and the tactics were different.

At first he spent a long time
on the substitute's bench at Leeds.

Eric playing his first match for Leeds United in 1992.

When at last he did play,
Cantona scored important goals for Leeds,
and helped them win the League that season.

Manchester United came a close second.

In the Charity Shield match
at the start of the 92–93 season,
Cantona scored a hat-trick,
as Leeds beat Liverpool 4–3.

Cantona's first full season in England
got off to the best possible start.

But it wasn't to last.

6 More problems

The problem was Leeds' away form.
Cantona was playing well
(he got another hat-trick
as Leeds beat Spurs 5–0).
But they kept throwing away the lead
in too many matches.
By the end of the season
Leeds were fighting to avoid relegation.

In the face of defeat,
Cantona began to sulk and lose his temper.
He missed training,
and was late for team meetings.
His new manager,
Howard Wilkinson,
was not prepared to stand any nonsense
from his hot-headed star.

He told Cantona off
in front of the other players,
just to hurt the Frenchman's pride.
He dropped Cantona from important matches,
and began to think about selling him.
He needed to get back
the money he'd paid out,
eleven months before,
to the French club, Nimes.

7 Manchester United

Eric Cantona signed for Manchester United
on November 26, 1992.
The fee was £1 million.

Perhaps manager Alex Ferguson
wondered if there was trouble ahead.

But he knew, inside himself,
it was the best £1 million he'd ever spend.

He said,
'I was told I was taking a risk,
but you gamble on every player:
You may as well gamble on one
who lifts people out of their seats.'

For a while, everything went well.
United had a run of 11 games
without a defeat.

Cantona settled in well,
he was scoring goals
and making goals for his team mates.

Then came United's next match.
It was against Leeds.

Eric scoring a goal for Manchester United in 1993.

The fans that had cheered Cantona
when he was a Leeds player
now jeered and hissed at him,
and spat at the other United players.

Cantona was stung by their laughter and hate.

He was booked for elbowing a Leeds player.
He was accused of spitting at Leeds fans
as he left the field at the end of the match.

The FA fined him £1,000,
and he was banned for two months.

The United manager Alex Ferguson
and all the United players
still believed in Cantona.

As soon as the ban was over
he was back in the team,
and United were back to their winning ways.

That season, United won the league.

Eric now had two Championship medals,
one for Leeds, one for United.

Not bad for 18 months' work!

Manchester United, League Champions 1993–4.

Next season,
United fought hard to win the League again.

But whenever they lost
or had a set-back,
there was Cantona, getting into trouble again.

He got a red card
in a European match in Turkey.
Then two yellow cards
and a five-match ban
for bad tackles against Norwich and Arsenal.

Then a red card
for stamping on a Swindon player.

The press were hard on Cantona,
calling him 'Mad Eric'.

But Alex Ferguson defended his star player:

'If Cantona has a weakness, it's his tackling . . .
I've told him: don't bother tackling,
or you'll end up getting a booking.'

Ferguson knew he needed the Frenchman.
All that season,
whenever Cantona played for United,
they lost only two matches.

When he didn't play,
they lost two out of three matches.

That year United won the Double,
the League Championship
and the FA Cup,
and Cantona was voted Player of the Year.

In United's next season, 1994–95,
Cantona missed 29 games.

United lost in Europe,
lost 1–0 to Everton in the final of the FA Cup,
and lost the League as well.
United came second,
a point behind Blackburn Rovers.

They needed something extra.

They needed Cantona,
but he was out of action,
banned for nine months
and fined over £20,000
after his attack
on a Crystal Palace fan
at Selhurst Park.

There was worse to come.

On March 23, 1995,
Cantona had to go to the magistrate's court
charged with assault
for his attack on the Palace fan,
Matthew Simmons.

8 In court

In court, the whole story came out:
how Simmons had shouted at Cantona
as he left the field.

Cantona said, 'He was shouting
in abusive, insulting and racist
or nationalistic terms.
I was obviously hurt, and . . .
I reacted in a way I now deeply regret . . .

'I should not have done this . . .'

The magistrate said
Cantona should set an example.

'You are a high-profile public figure . . .
and you are looked up to
by many young people.'

She sentenced him
to two weeks in prison.

A Crown Court judge changed this sentence
to 120 hours community service.

Over the next nine months,
Eric would teach his footballing skills
to over 600 school children.

Eric coming out of court in 1995.

Meanwhile, Matthew Simmons
had to go to court
for shouting at Cantona
and causing the trouble
in the first place.

Simmons also lacked discipline.
He attacked and punched the people
who were arguing against him,
when the court found him guilty!

Was it the end of Eric Cantona?
Would Eric want to stay in English football?

Would Manchester United want to keep him?
Alex Ferguson had a lot of thinking to do.

Maybe he should sell Cantona to Inter Milan.
They were very keen to buy him,
ban or no ban.
Inter offered £5 million to buy Cantona.
His pay would be £25,000 a week.

But Ferguson said no.
Instead of Cantona,
he sold Paul Ince to Inter,
for nearly £8 million.
Kanchelskis and Mark Hughes
were sold as well.

Alex Ferguson was building a new team.
Eric Cantona was the centre of attention!

Eric told the press,

'I'm very pleased to have the opportunity
to win many trophies with Manchester United.
Everyone at the club deserves this,
and the fans too.'

Then he added,

'I can forget everything now . . .
even the criticism;
because I know we can win everything.'

9 Cantona the man

Eric may have been a hot-head
on the football field.
But at home he has a quiet family life.

He married his wife Isabelle in 1986.
They have a son called Raphael
who was born in 1988.
They also have a daughter called Josephine
who was born in 1995.
Isabelle is expecting their third child soon.
They live in Prestbury.
Eric is often seen
collecting Raphael from school.

Eric likes to keep his family away from
photographers and reporters.
His family life is private and
it is rare to see a picture of Eric and his family.

Eric likes art and painting.
He also likes reading, and writing poetry.
His father liked the same things.

He has been seen
in a French-style cafe in Manchester,
playing chess
and talking about chess moves.

Cantona has acted in TV advertisements
for Nike and Eurostar.
(Eurostar runs trains to France from England.)

These advertisements show the two sides of
Cantona.

Nike show him, with other football stars,
on the field of battle.
The battle is between Good and Evil.

Eurostar shows Eric as a man of culture,
travelling to France on the train.
He is shown talking about philosophy.

Sometimes Eric's philosophy is hard to follow.
After the Crystal Palace court case
he said to the press,

'When the sea-gulls follow the fishing boat,
it is because they think
that sardines will be thrown into the sea.'

He wasn't talking about Crystal Palace,
or about Matthew Simmons,
or even about football.
He was talking about fame.

But many people are still trying to work out
just what Eric is going on about.
He doesn't help people understand.
In fact, even Alex Ferguson has said
'I'm lucky if he speaks to me'.

10 Changed for good

The next season, 95–96,
as soon as the Crystal Palace ban was over,
Cantona was back.

And when Steve Bruce was sold,
Cantona was made captain.

He led United to win the Double again.

They caught Newcastle United
who had been 12 points clear,
to win the League Championship.

Then Cantona scored the goal that beat Liverpool
late in the FA Cup Final.

And he was voted Player of the Year
for the second time in three years.

The Selhurst Park incident
changed Cantona for good.
His attitude,
both on and off the field,
could not be better.
There were no fights,
no sly kicks, no stamping.

He'd really paid back the faith
that Alex Ferguson
and the United players had in him!

Eric and Alex Ferguson show off the FA Cup and the
Premier League Trophy, 1996.

Where can Eric Cantona go from here?

He's already won everything in Britain.
Now, his greatest ambition
must be to win in Europe.

There are the big European competitions:
The European Cup,
the UEFA Cup,
the Cup Winner's Cup.

This ambition is shared by Alex Ferguson too.
The Manchester United manager
would love to win the European Cup,
and now he wants Cantona to win it for him.

Can Cantona and Manchester United do it?